Seasonal Crafts
Autumn

Gillian · Chapman

WAYLAND

500587443

Seasonal Crafts

Spring • Summer • Autumn • Winter

Series editor: Sarah Doughty
Design and artwork by Gillian Chapman
DTP design by Joyce Chester

First published in 1997 by Wayland Publishers Ltd
61 Western Road, Hove, East Sussex, BN3 1JD

British Library Cataloguing in Publication Data
Chapman, Gillian
    Autumn. – (Seasonal crafts)
    1. Holiday decorations – Juvenile literature 2. Handicraft –
    Juvenile literature
    I. Title
    745.5'941

ISBN 0 7502 1839 8

Printed and bound by G. Canale & C.S.p.A., Borgaro Tse,
Turin

Picture acknowledgements:
Bruce Coleman Ltd 4 (Jane Burton); Eye Ubiquitous 12 (Chris
Bland); Galaxy Picture Library 28 (Robin Scagell); Sally and
Richard Greenhill 20; Impact 22 (Peter Arkell); Photri 6; Tony
Stone Worldwide 16 (J. F. Preedy), 24 (David Young Woolff),
26 (David Hiser); Wayland Picture Library 10; Zefa 8, 14, 18.

All commissioned photography, including the cover pictures
by Chris Fairclough. Props made by Gillian Chapman.

Contents

Words that are shown in **bold** are explained in the glossary on page 31.

Autumn Colours

△ *A grey squirrel gathers hazelnuts together for its winter store.*

Autumn is a season of great activity. It is the time to get ready for the winter months ahead. Some animals gather food and store it away for winter. Some birds fly away to warmer places. The days begin to get colder and shorter. Trees and plants shed their leaves and seeds, and these give the countryside the beautiful colours of autumn.

Fruit and cereal crops are harvested in autumn. It is a season of **celebration**, when people give thanks for a good harvest.

Autumn Projects

Autumn seeds, leaves and other natural materials make exciting collages. Collect them on a dry day, only taking those that have fallen to the ground. At home, arrange your collection on newspaper, allowing them to fully dry out before starting work.

Starting Work

All materials and equipment needed for each project are listed on each page. An adult's help may be useful with some cutting and gluing.

Recycling Materials

Many of the materials needed to make the projects in this book are free! Start to collect clean scrap paper, card, magazines and empty boxes – they will all be useful.

Use old newspaper and rags for covering work surfaces and for mopping up. Plastic containers of all sizes are handy for water and for mixing paint.

Paints and Glues

Poster and powder paints are ideal for most craftwork, but thicker poster paint or ready-mixed paint is better for splattering and printing. A selection of different sized paint brushes is useful, and felt pens are perfect for fine detail.

Keep old brushes separate for gluing. PVA glue will stick large collage materials, like seeds, leaves and thick cardboard. Use a glue stick for paper and thin card.

The Fall

Autumn is the time of the year when some types of trees shed their leaves and seeds. In America, the season of autumn is called 'the Fall' because it is when leaves die and fall to the ground.

Leaves make sugar for the tree to feed on during the winter. On very cold, frosty nights the sugar cannot pass into the branches. It collects in the dying leaves, giving them their brilliant colours.

During the Fall the colours of the trees change to reds, yellows, oranges and browns. ▽

Making Splatter Prints

Autumn Gift Wrap

1 First cover the work surface with plenty of newspaper. Place a sheet of paper in the centre and arrange the leaves on top.

2 Mix some thick paint and dip the toothbrush into it. Run an old pencil across the bristles, splattering paint over the paper and leaves. Let the paint dry before lifting off the leaves. △

You will need:
* Dry autumn leaves
* Newspaper
* Sheets of paper
* Thin card
* Poster paints and brush
* Scissors and pencil
* Old toothbrush
* Old pencil or stick
* Scraps of ribbon

Autumn Leaf Cards

1 Place a large leaf on to card and draw around it with the pencil. Then cut out the shape. ▽

2 Put the leaf shape on the newspaper and splatter it with paint. When the paint is dry, fold the leaf in half. Large leaves make attractive greetings cards. Thread the small ones with ribbon to make gift tags.

7

Chinese Kite Festival

The Chinese have been flying kites for thousands of years. They are usually made from materials like bamboo, silk and paper which are all very light. The weathermen of Ancient China **forecast** a wind from the east in early September. This made it a perfect time of year to hold a festival for kite flying.

On the last day of the festival Chinese children have a holiday from school to fly their kites. At the end of the day they cut the kite strings and let them fly away.

Preparing a kite for a child to fly at the Chinese Kite Festival. ▽

Making a Paper Kite

1 Position the three plant sticks across each other, as shown, and tie them together with string.

2 Place them on top of a sheet of paper cut to the same size as the stick framework. ▽

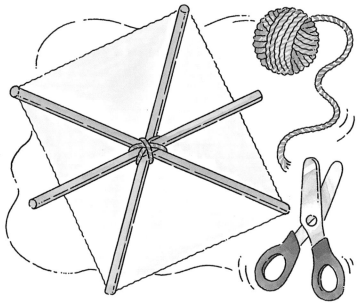

4 Turn the kite over and paint a fearsome face on the front.

5 Tie a long length of string to the crossbar and attach this line to the bamboo cane. You can fly the kite by holding the cane up high and running along. ▽

3 Using strips of strong sticky tape, attach the paper to the sticks at the four corners. ▽

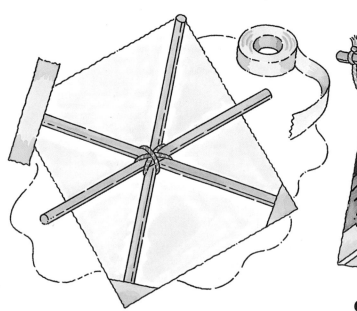

Back to School

In many countries children go back to school at the beginning of autumn after the summer holidays. For most children it is the start of a new school year with new teachers, new topics, new books and equipment.

Get ready for school with these two simple projects, using up scraps of card and coloured paper. Make a bookmark to match the story you are reading and tidy up your desk with an animal letter rack.

Children at this school are all working together on a new project. ▽

Making Animal Bookmarks and Letter Racks

1 To make a bookmark cut two slits in the piece of card. ▽

1 To make a letter rack, cut off the top and sides of a cereal box. ▽

2 Cut some animal shapes and features from coloured paper and glue them to the top of the bookmark. △

2 Paint the box and decorate it with scraps of coloured card cut into animal shapes. ▽

3 Slot the bookmark over the page in your book. Then you won't lose your place. △

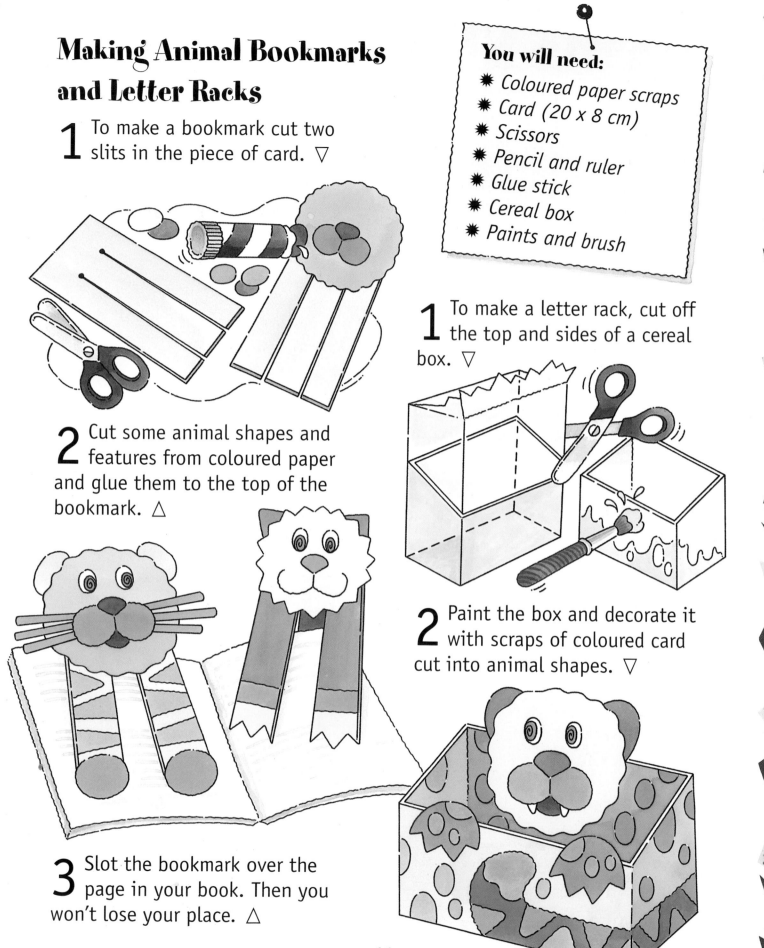

11

Harvest Time

△ *This French farmer will be celebrating a very successful grape harvest.*

All around the world people celebrate harvest and give thanks for good crops. A good grape harvest means much merry-making in all countries that make wines. In Japan there is a rice harvest festival and in West Africa the yam harvest is celebrated with dancing and mask making.

Many religions hold special harvest festivals of thanksgiving. Christians bring bread, fruit and vegetables into their churches to be **blessed**. Jewish families celebrate the end of harvest with the festival of **Succot**.

Making a Harvest Mask

1 Cut a circle out of the card, using a dinner plate as a template. △

2 Hold the card circle in front of your face and ask an adult to mark the position of your eyes and mouth. Then cut out the holes. (You may need some help with this.) △

3 Tape a stick to the back of the mask to support it. △

4 Cover the front of the card with glue. Working from the outside overlap leaves, grasses and seeds until the card is covered. ▽

13

Migration

Large numbers of birds do not stay for the cold winter. They **migrate** and fly thousands of kilometres to spend the winter in warmer places.

Swallows, swifts, wild ducks and geese all migrate. They travel to the same place every year and return home in the spring to **breed**. The birds fly by day and night, possibly using the sun and stars to guide them. Some insects, such as butterflies, also migrate.

A flock of geese fly away across a beautiful autumn sky to find a warmer place for the winter. ▽

Making a Flapping Bird Mobile

You will need:
* 30 cm long plant stick
* Coloured card
* Felt pens
* Scissors
* Crêpe paper scraps
* Thread
* Hole punch

1 Cut out some bird shapes from the coloured card. Make a slot in the birds' bodies and decorate the birds with felt pens. △

2 Pleat a strip of crêpe paper to make the wings and thread them through the slot. △

3 Punch a hole in each bird and tie a piece of thread through. Tie the thread to the stick, making the birds hang at different heights. △

4 Tie a length of thread to each end of the stick. Hang the mobile by an open window and watch the birds fly in the breeze. ▽

15

Hibernation

Autumn is a busy time for animals as they get ready for winter. They look for safe hiding places to store nuts and seeds. They build nests and grow thicker coats. Frogs, lizards and snakes bury themselves in underground holes away from the frost. Snails huddle together under stones.

Some animals, like bats, dormice and hamsters **hibernate** through the winter. During the autumn they eat plenty of food to help them through the long months of rest. When they hibernate their body temperature falls and their heartbeat is very slow.

A dormouse hibernates, safely curled up in a warm nest of dried grass. ▽

Making an Animal Pencil Holder

You will need:

* Card tube
* Coloured paper scraps
* Thin card
* Scissors
* Glue stick
* Felt pens

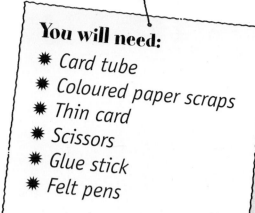

1 Cover the card tube with coloured paper. Line up the top of the tube with the edge of the paper and glue it in place. △

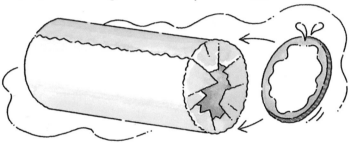

2 Tuck any extra paper into the bottom of the tube. Cut out a circle of card and glue it to the base of the tube. △

3 Cut out two identical animal shapes from the card. These will need to be large enough to glue halfway around the tube, and to each other. △

4 Glue the animal shapes in place using the glue stick. Decorate the pencil holder with scraps of coloured paper and felt pens. ▽

Autumn Animals

△ *The dappled brown feathers of this pin-tailed sandgrouse camouflage it amongst the dried leaves and grasses.*

In autumn the colours of the countryside change from greens to golden browns. Fallen leaves and seeds lie on the ground.

Animals and birds such as rabbits, pheasants, mice and snakes are **camouflaged** against these autumn colours. Some animals change the colour of their coats when the season changes. In winter the stoat and mountain hare **moult**. Their brown summer fur changes to white so that they blend in with the snow around them.

Making a Camouflage Collage

1 Glue the long box to the bottom edge of a piece of stiff card, using the PVA glue. ▽

You will need:
* Feathers, dry leaves, twigs and seeds
* PVA glue and brush
* 2 pieces of stiff card
* Long box
* Scissors
* Brown paint and brush

2 Paint the box brown and let it dry. Then make an autumn collage with the natural materials you have collected. Cover the card, gluing the collage in place with PVA. ▽

3 Draw an animal shape on the other piece of card and cut it out. Decorate the shape with the rest of the natural materials, gluing them to the card with PVA. △

4 When the animal collage is dry, glue it to the front of the box. The collage will now stand up. The animal will be well camouflaged against the background of natural materials. ▷

Diwali

The festival of Diwali is the beginning of the Hindu New Year. Hindus remember the ancient story of Rama and Sita who were **banished** from their kingdom for 14 years. Rama came back and killed the evil ten-headed **demon** king Ravana. Rama was made king.

Diwali means 'row of lights' and Hindus place small oil lamps, called **divas**, in their windows to guide Rama and Sita home. Families celebrate Diwali by holding fireworks parties and giving each other presents.

All Hindu families come together to celebrate Diwali or the 'Festival of Light'. ▽

Making Festive Lanterns

1 Cut your sheet of paper to the same length as a jam jar and cut off the rest. △

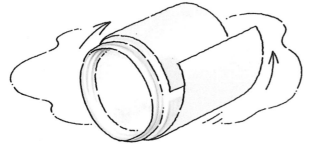

2 Wrap the paper around the jar to make sure it is long enough to cover it and allow for a 2 cm overlap. △

3 Paint patterns on the paper. When the paint dries punch holes in the paper for the night light to shine through. ▽

4 Wrap the decorated paper around the jar and stick it in place with the tape. Tie a string handle to the rim of the jar. ◁

✋ Ask an adult to place a night light in the jar and to light it. NEVER leave the lanterns unattended when they are alight.

United Nations Day

△ *By planting a tree these children are helping to make their world a better place to live in.*

The United Nations (UN) was formed on 24 October 1945. The world had been at war for more than five years and now the UN wanted to help keep world peace. Every year on this day people think about peace around the world.

The UN organized the The Earth Summit, held in 1992 in Rio de Janeiro. More than 150 governments agreed to a set of laws, called Agenda 21. These laws will try and help to save our planet from war and **pollution** as we move into the next century.

Making a Peace Collage

1 Look through your collection of old magazines and comics and cut out all the pictures that make you think of peace. ▽

You will need:
* ✻ Large piece of card
* ✻ Old magazines
* ✻ Glue stick
* ✻ Scissors
* ✻ Pencil
* ✻ Coloured paper

2 Arrange the pictures on a large piece of stiff card. Glue them in place with the glue stick. △

3 Pleat a piece of coloured paper. Draw a simple outline of a figure on the paper and cut it out, making sure you cut through all the layers.

4 Carefully unfold the row of figures and cut out several more in different colours. Glue the figures along the edge of your collage. They show people around the world joining together for peace.

Hallowe'en

△ *On the night of Hallowe'en children dress up ready for fun!*

Hallowe'en is the night for dressing up and making mischief! Children sometimes play 'trick or treat' games with their friends.

Long ago, the **Celts** celebrated their New Year's Eve on this night with great feasts and dancing. They lit huge bonfires to frighten away the ghosts and evil spirits that they believed were **haunting** them.

This day was made into a Christian festival and is known as the eve of All Hallow's or All Saints' Day.

Making Scary Spiders

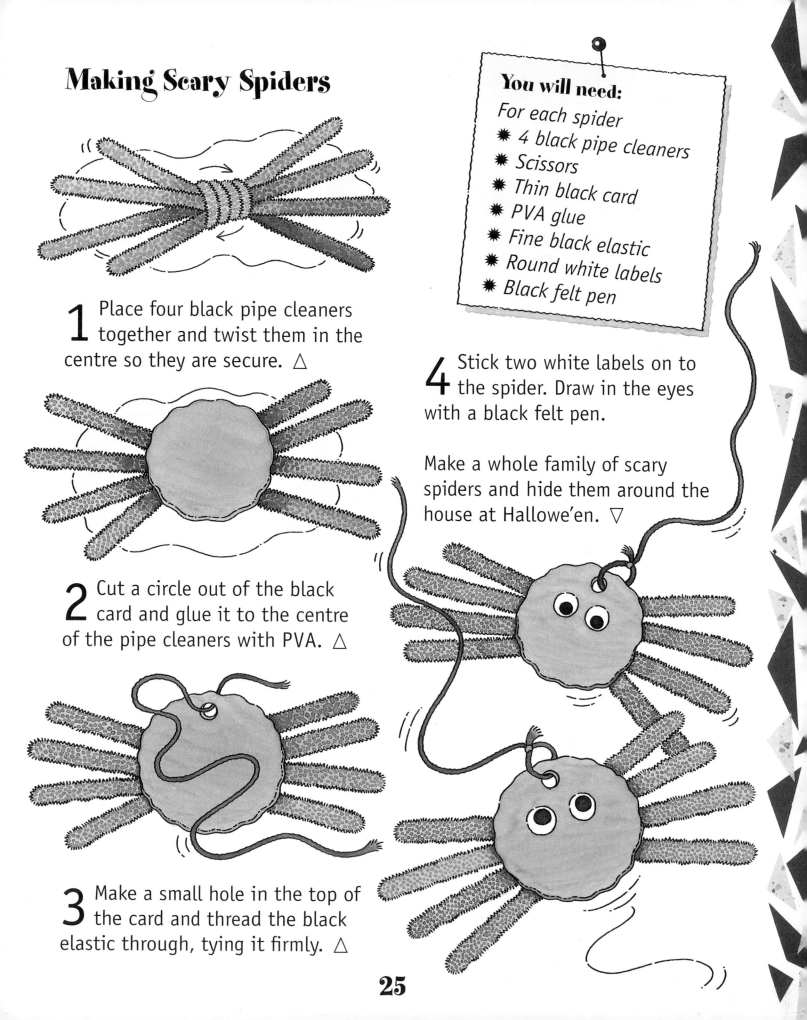

1 Place four black pipe cleaners together and twist them in the centre so they are secure. △

2 Cut a circle out of the black card and glue it to the centre of the pipe cleaners with PVA. △

3 Make a small hole in the top of the card and thread the black elastic through, tying it firmly. △

4 Stick two white labels on to the spider. Draw in the eyes with a black felt pen.

Make a whole family of scary spiders and hide them around the house at Hallowe'en. ▽

All Souls' Day

△ *Mexican people make large skeleton puppets to dance in the Day of the Dead celebrations.*

This is the day when Christians remember their family and friends who have died. Some people believe that on this day the souls return to earth to visit their old homes.

In Mexico it is known as the Day of the Dead and is an important religious festival. People parade in the streets in colourful costumes and perform masked dances. Mexican families leave cakes and flowers on the graves to welcome their souls back home on this special day.

Making a Skeleton Puppet

1 Cut up the card to make the main pieces for the puppet. You will need a rectangle for the body, a circle for the head and four long strips for the arms and legs. △

2 Place the pieces together and paint a skeleton on them. You may need to look at a picture of a skeleton in a book. ▽

4 Punch a hole in the top of the skull and in each hand. Thread a length of string through each and tie them to the lolly stick. Now your skeleton is ready to dance! ▽

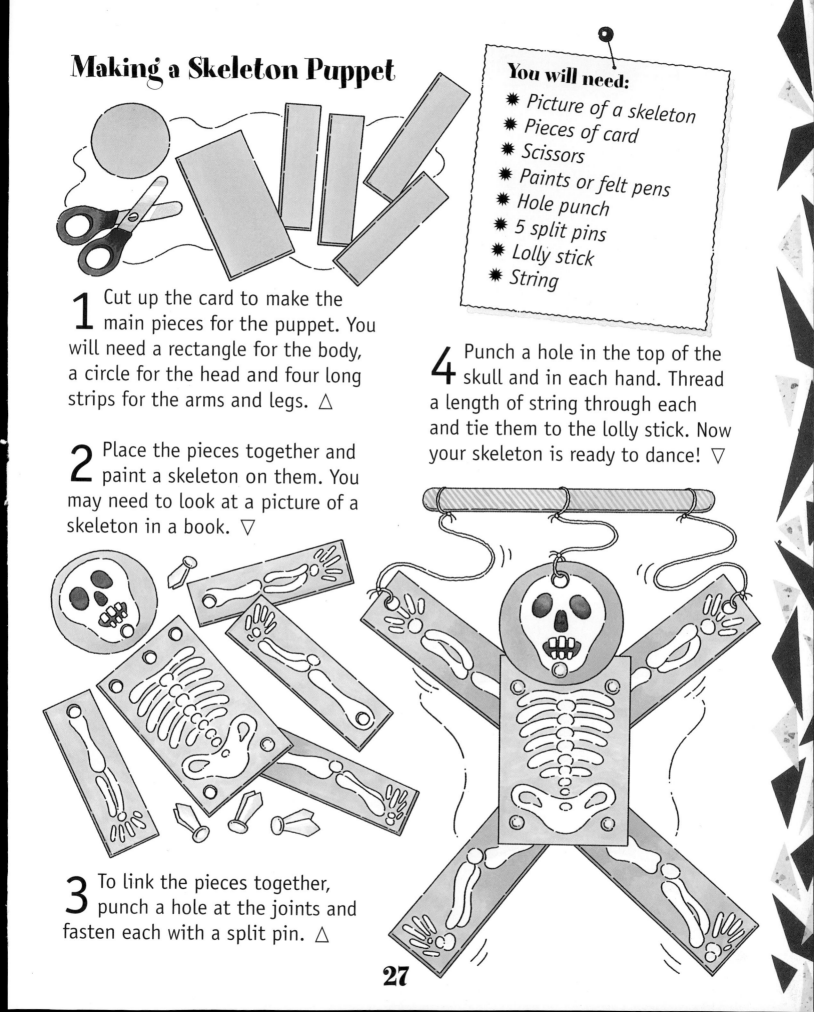

3 To link the pieces together, punch a hole at the joints and fasten each with a split pin. △

Autumn Stars

A clear autumn night is a good time to look at the stars. Groups of stars are called constellations. The Ancient Greeks saw groups of stars as pictures in the sky. They named these groups of stars after creatures or people from their own **legends**.

There is a group of stars called Ursa Major, which means 'The Great Bear' and another called Scorpius, who was the scorpion that stung **Orion** to death. Look in a book about the night sky to find out more about constellations.

A group of stars called the Plough, or Big Dipper, can be seen clearly in the autumn sky. It is part of the Great Bear constellation. ▽

Making Star Cards

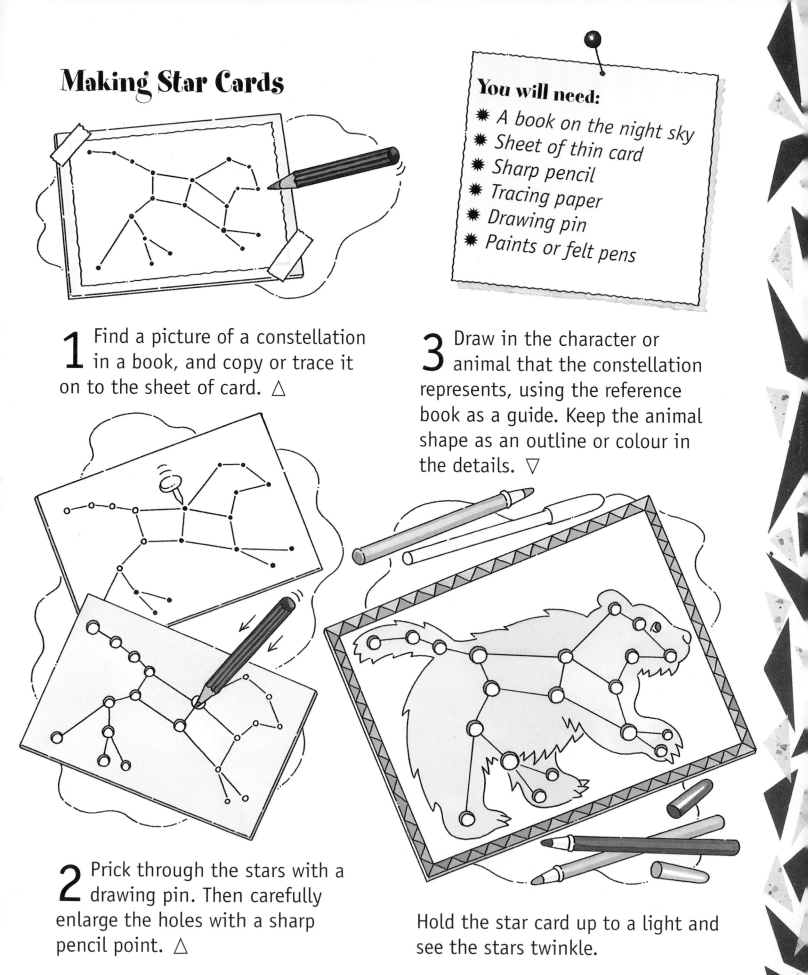

You will need:
* A book on the night sky
* Sheet of thin card
* Sharp pencil
* Tracing paper
* Drawing pin
* Paints or felt pens

1 Find a picture of a constellation in a book, and copy or trace it on to the sheet of card. △

2 Prick through the stars with a drawing pin. Then carefully enlarge the holes with a sharp pencil point. △

3 Draw in the character or animal that the constellation represents, using the reference book as a guide. Keep the animal shape as an outline or colour in the details. ▽

Hold the star card up to a light and see the stars twinkle.

Autumn Calendar

This calendar refers only to events and festivals mentioned in this book.

Chinese Kite Festival
1–9 September
Succot (The Jewish Feast of Tabernacles)
September or October
Harvest Time
Mid-October in Britain, US and other Western countries
United Nations Day
Late October
Diwali (The Hindu Festival of Light)
October or early November
Hallowe'en
31 October
All Saints' Day
1 November
All Souls' Day
2 November

Many religions and cultures use the lunar calendar, which mean that their festivals are not held on the same day every year.

Glossary

banished To be thrown out of your country against your will.

blessed When a religious person has asked for God's favour.

breed To give birth to young.

camouflaged To be hidden against a similar background.

Celts A race of people who live in northern Europe.

celebration A special happy event or festival.

demon A wicked being or spirit.

divas A Hindu word for small clay oil lamps.

forecasted To have worked out what will happen in the future.

haunting Frightening and worrying.

hibernate To spend the winter in a deep sleep.

legends Stories from the past.

migrate To move from one place to another, over a long distance.

moult When animals lose their fur coat or skin.

Orion A Roman god, who has a star constellation named after him.

pollution Spoiling the land, sea or air and making it dirty.

Succot Festival which remembers the Jews' search for a homeland.

Books to Read

Information Series

Blueprints *series* (Stanley Thornes)
    especially *Seasonal Topics* and
    Festivals
My Belief *series* (Franklin Watts)
Our Culture *series* (Franklin Watts)
World-wide Crafts *series* (A & C
    Black) especially *Celebrations* by
    Chris Deshpande

Craft series, including Seasons

First Arts and Crafts *series* (Wayland)
Go, Set, Go! *series* (Franklin Watts)
Seasonal Projects *series* (Wayland)
Starting Points *series* (Franklin Watts)

For festival poster: The Festival Shop,
56 Poplar Road, King's Heath,
Birmingham B14 7AG.

Index